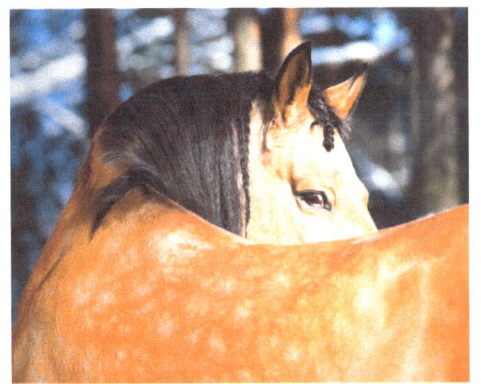

Shire horse

HORSE
& Mule

Images for Artist's Reference & Inspiration

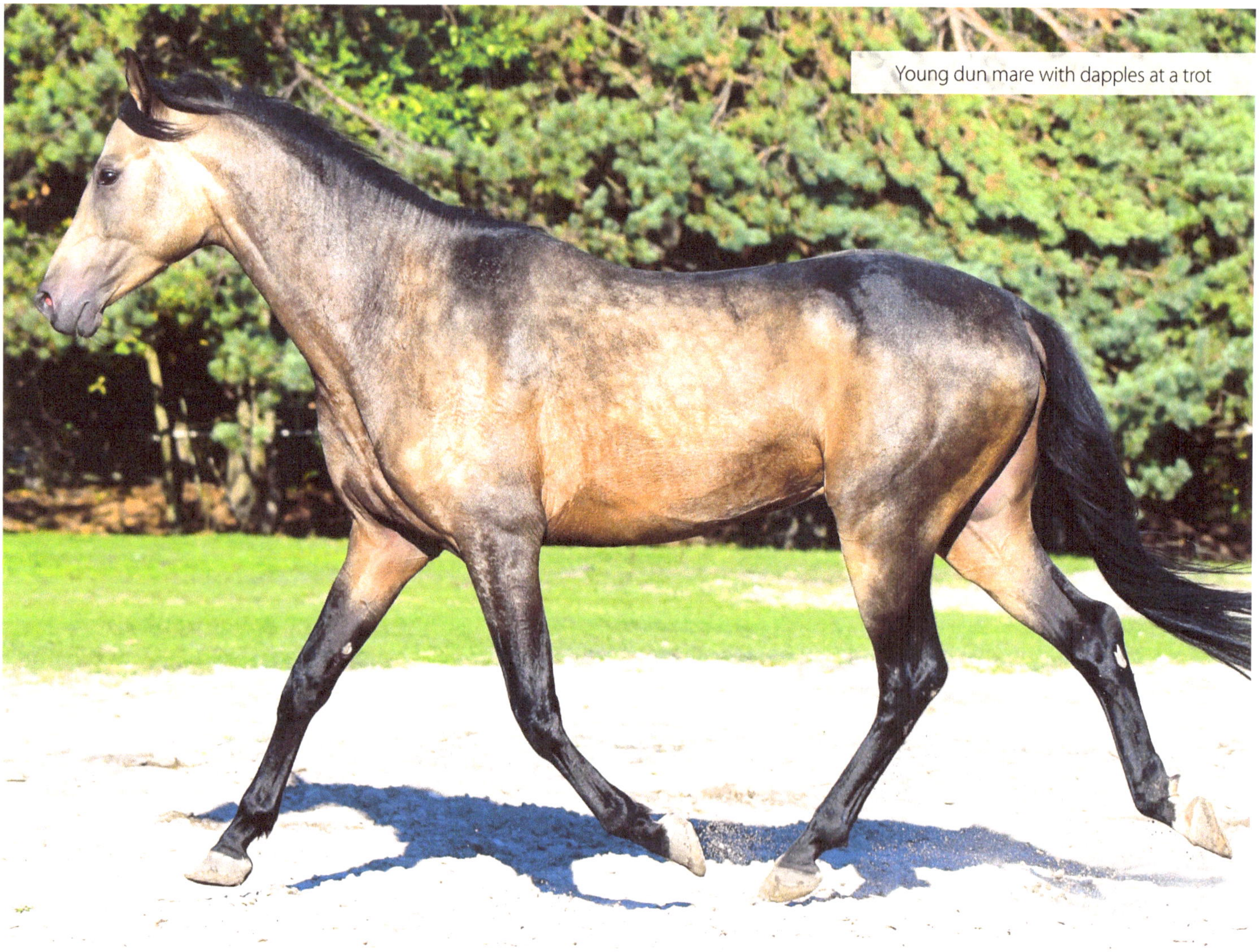

Young dun mare with dapples at a trot

Table of Contents

I would like to thank all of the talented photographers from around the globe who have made their work available on Dreamstime, Adobe Stock, and in the public domain. Their talent has made this book possible. A big thank you goes out to David Dineen and to Karen and Kara Prescott.

If you have purchased this book and would like to view, download, or purchase these photographs for your drawing, sculpting, or model horse show reference needs, please visit Dreamstime.com, stock.adobe.com, or Creative Commons.

Same dun mare as above

Same gelding as right

Rearing grulla Bashkir horse gelding

Grulla Bashkir mare and bay stallion

Grulla Bashkir gelding at a canter

Dark dapple gray gelding

Dapple gray gelding at a canter

Dapple gray Arabian

Same Arabian

Light dapple gray Welsh Mountain Pony Mare

Medium dapple gray Welsh Mountain Pony

Dark dapple gray mare and her muddy filly

Dark dapple gray mare and her filly at a canter

3

Rose gray Arabian mare

Rose gray Arabian mare with dark points

Dapple gray Arabian stallion (racing type)

Light rose gray Arabian at a canter

Dapple gray Arabian Stallion

Dapple gray Arabian Stallion

Rose gray Arabian Stallion

Young chestnut Arabian Gelding at a trot

Bay Arabian Stallion

Stallion wearing a traditional saddle for a
Fantasia/*lab el baroud* performance, Morocco

Fantasia/*lab el baroud* performance horse,
of Arabian, Andalusian, or Barb breeding

Chestnut Arabian mare

Chestnut Arabian mare at trot

Bay Arabian stallion

Bay Peruvian Paso mare performing the paso llano gait

Missouri Foxtrotter stallion

Young chestnut Peruvian Paso mare performing paso llano. Lima, Peru. Photo by Tomas Sobek.

Gray Lippizan gelding performing with rider

Lusitano gelding. Photo by Linda Stanley

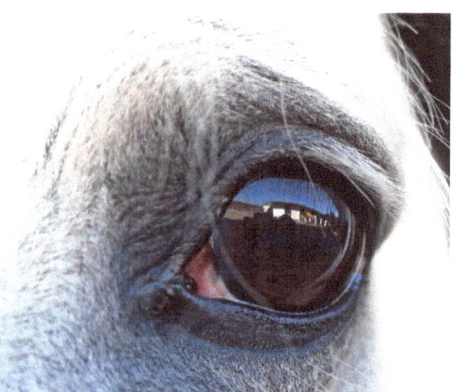

Flea-bitten gray Andalusian stallion at a trot

Gray Lippizan performing a Capriole. Photo by Bob Haarmans.

Photo by Bob Haarmans.

Gray Lippizan at a trot

Gray Lippizan at a walk

Gray Lippizan mare at a trot and her foal at a gallop. Photo by Bob Haarmans.

Chestnut Budonny mare

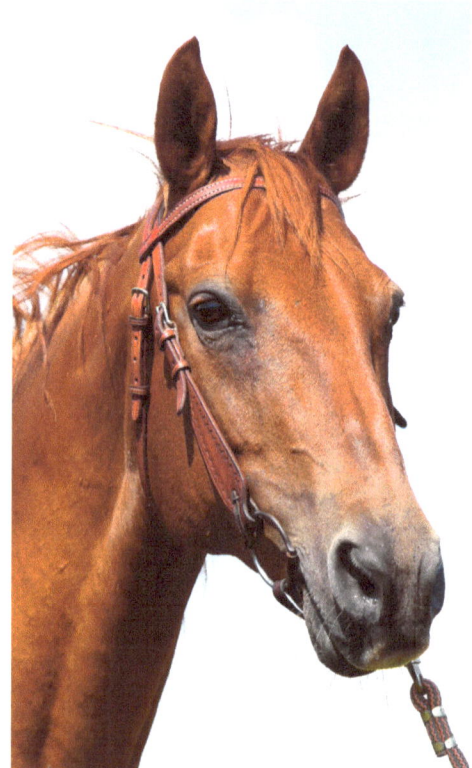

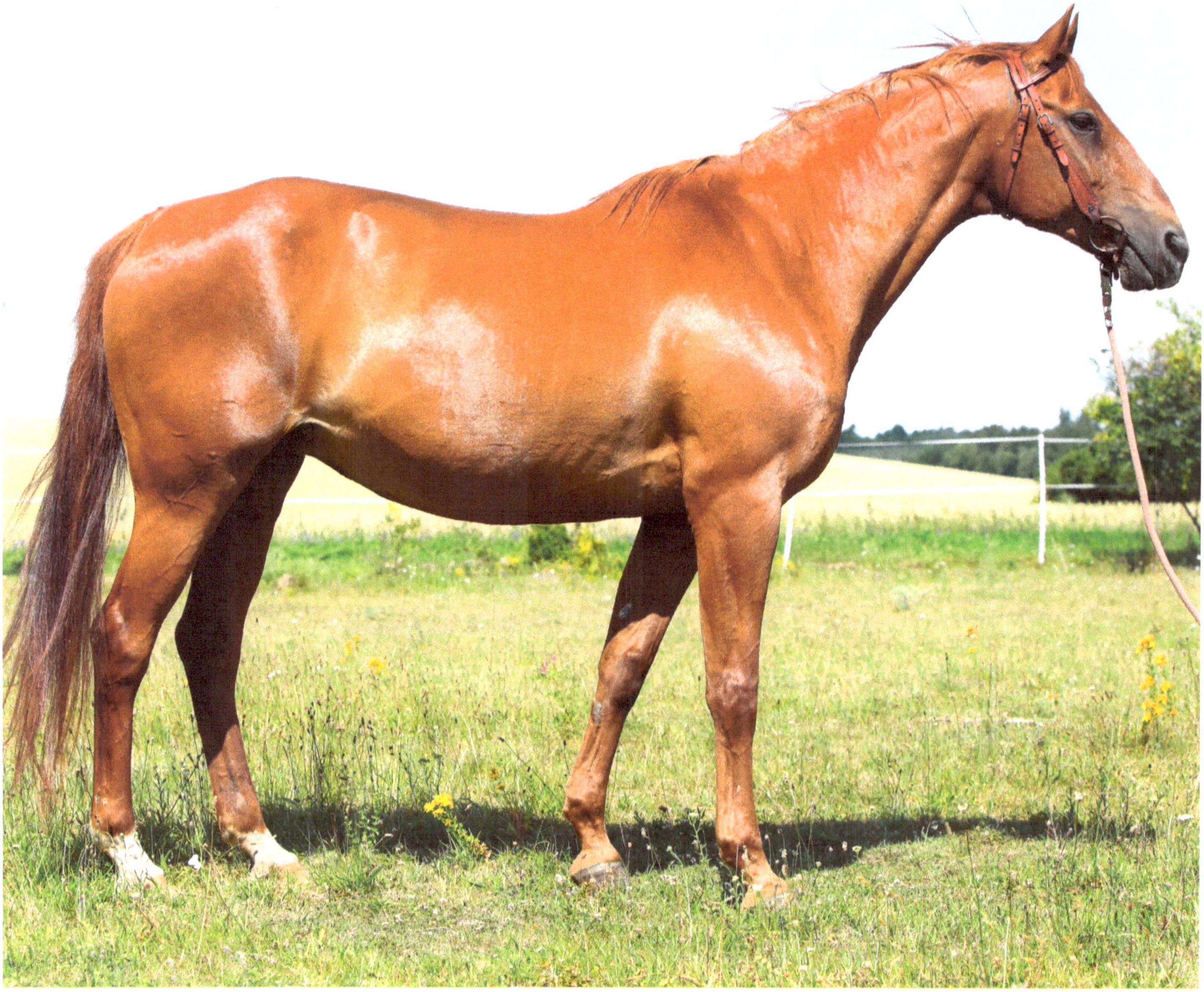

Young bay sport breed stallion

Bay Holsteiner mare at a trot

Dapple bay sport breed mare

Gelding, possibly a Knabstrupper, with Appaloosa coloring

Dapple chestnut sport breed stallion at a canter

Palomino warmblood gelding

At a canter

Buckskin Akhal Teke stallion

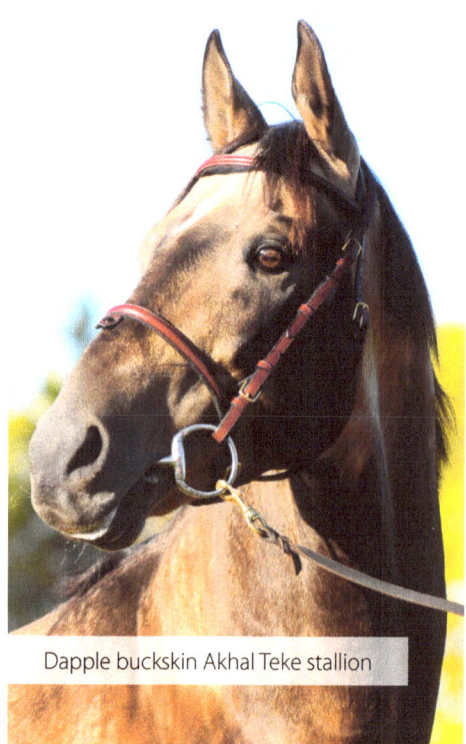

Dapple buckskin Akhal Teke stallion

Blue-eyed Akhal Teke geldings in smoky black and creamello

Chestnut Paint mare galloping

Bay Paint mare at a trot

Bay Paint mare at a trot

Bay Paint gelding at a canter

Palomino Paint mare at a canter

Bay Paint mare with blue eye at a canter

Dappled palomino Quarter Horse stallion

At a canter

Buckskin Quarter Horse gelding

Leopard Appaloosa mare

Leopard Appaloosa mare at a trot

Semi-leopard bay Appaloosa pony gelding with clipped coat

Arab/Appaloosa colt with blanket

Leopard Appaloosa

Bay pinto Irish Tinker/Gypsy Vanner mare

Red roan Belgian/Brabant Draft horse stallion

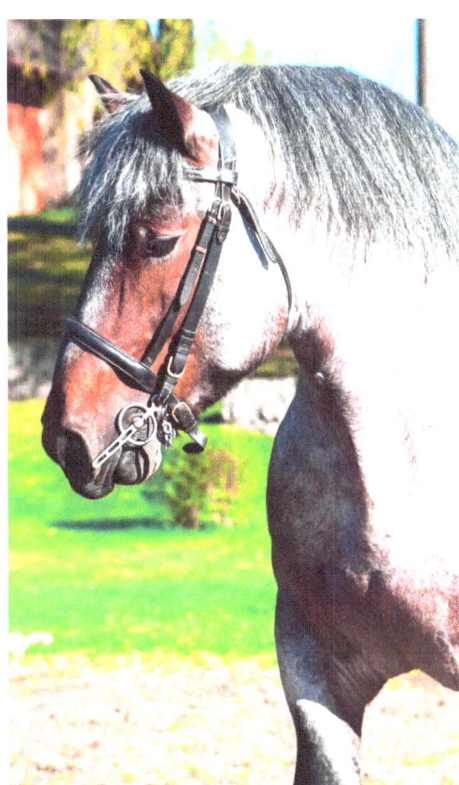

Dapple bay draft horse

At a trot

At a trot

At a canter

At a canter

Bay sabino Shire gelding

At a canter

Dapple sandy bay Irish Tinker/Gypsy Vanner

Buckskin Vladimir Heavy Draft

Buckskin Vladimir Heavy Draft stallion

Dapple pregnant mare, Pyrenees

Dapple draft horse mare

Dapple pregnant mare

Bay draft horse with pangare at a canter

Shire and miniature friends

Dapple gray Shire gelding

Belgian Draft Horse

Dapple liver chestnut draft horse stallion at a canter

At a trot

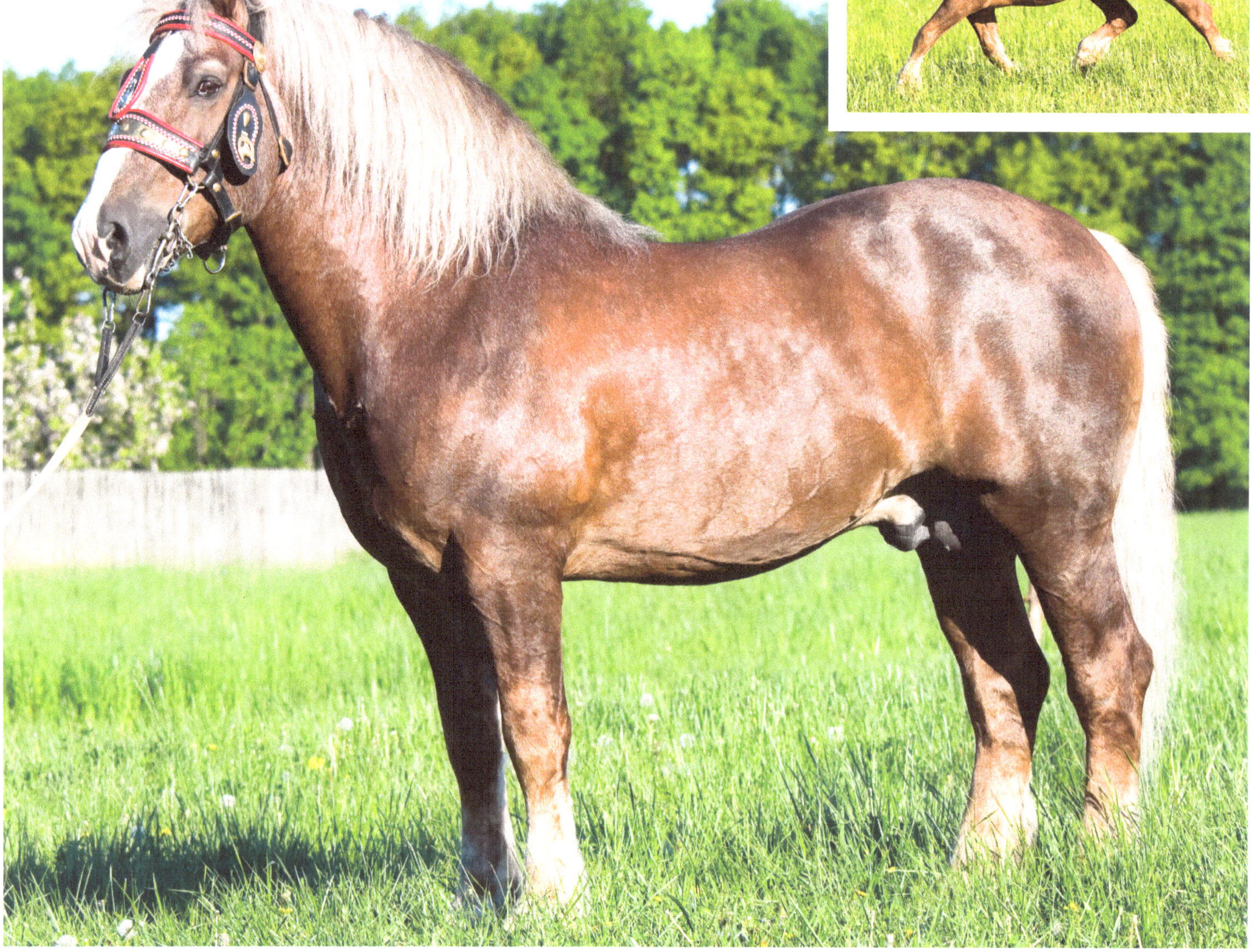

Bay Clydesdale gelding at canter

Various Friesians

Photo by Jean

Friesian at walk

Friesian Stallion at trot

Friesian stallion at trot

Friesian stallion at gallop

Friesian stallion at trot

Gray and dapple gray Camargue horses

Camargue horse at trot

Camargue horse at a canter

Gray and dapple gray Camargue horses

Muddy Camargue horses

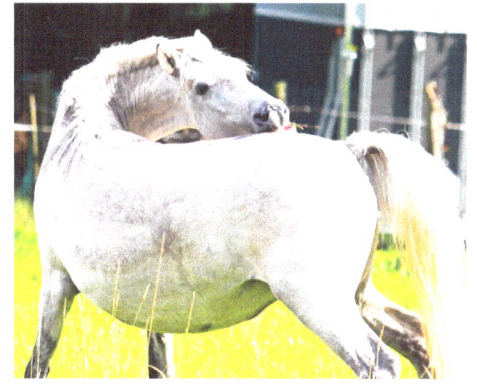

Wild Exmoor ponies in shades of bay

Exmoor pony mare in the show ring

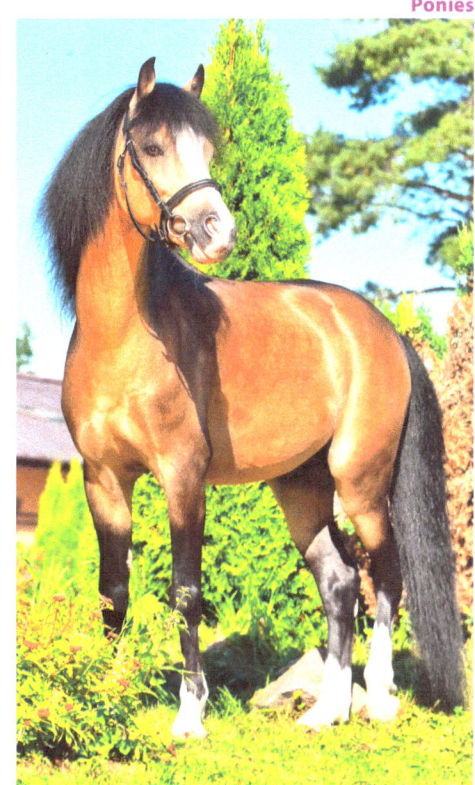

Dun Welsh Mountain Pony Stallion with dapples

Liver chestnut Welsh Cob stallion

Sorrel Haflinger stallion

at a walk

Liver chestnut Icelandic horse

Pinto Icelandic stallion

Grulla Icelandic horse

Cantering grulla Icelandic horse

Grulla Icelandic horse

Silver dapple Icelandic

Pregnant red dun Icelandic mare

Dapple Icelandic horse

Bay pinto pony gelding

At a canter

Sorrel pinto Icelandic

Sorrel pinto Icelandic

Sorrel pinto Icelandic

Dun Icelandic horse stallion

Appaloosa colored pony stallion at a canter

Shetland pony stallion

Palomino pinto miniature horse

Bay pinto miniature horse and playmate

Gray Welsh pony stallion

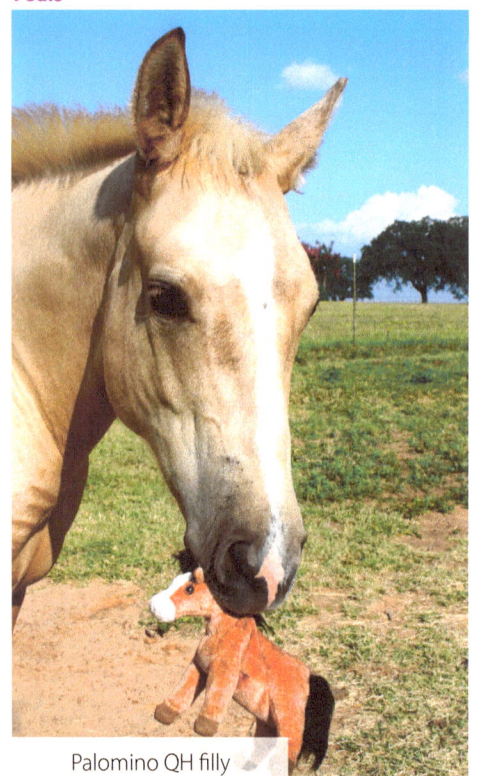

Palomino QH filly

Same palomino Quarter Horse filly with Pearlino dam at a trot

Bay miniature mule colt

Pinto Gypsy Vanner/Irish Tinker colt with one blue eye

Mini mule colt with dam

Akhal Teke filly at canter

Bay foal

Bay Akhal Teke filly at trot

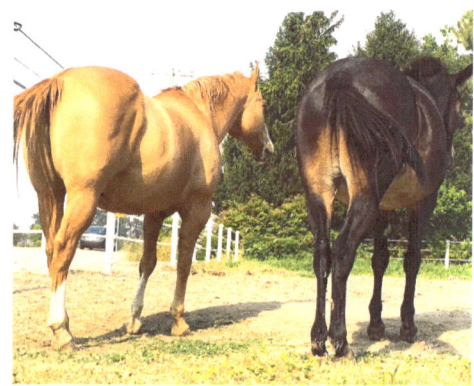

Small bay john and pony friend

Large bay molly mule

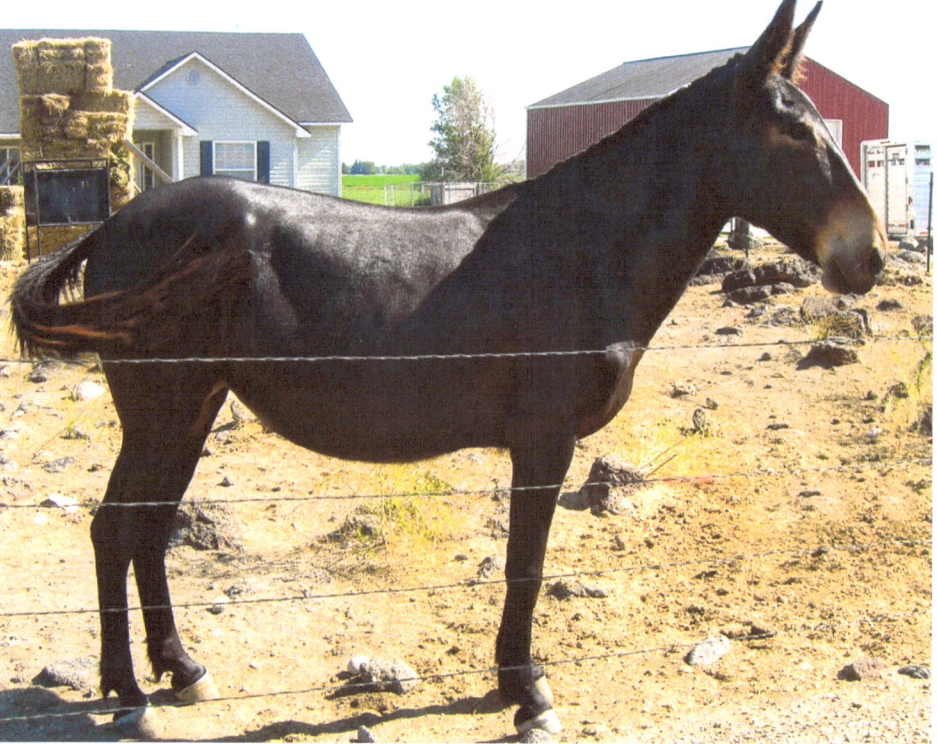

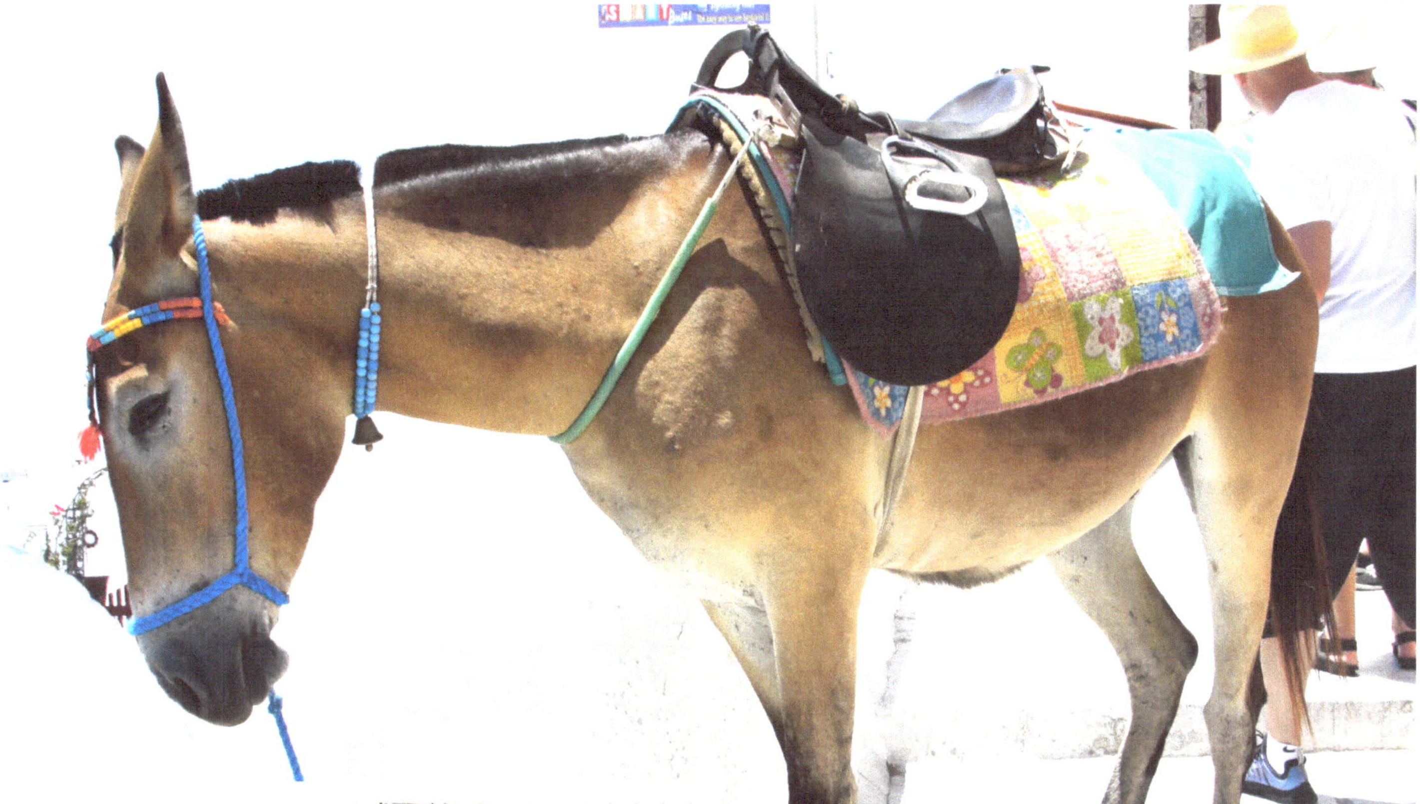

Buckskin mule, photo by Klearchos Kapoutsis,
Santorini, Greece

Buckskin mules,
photo by Norbert Nagar

Bay mules, photo by Mstyslav Chernov

Buckskin mule,
photo by Norbert Nagar

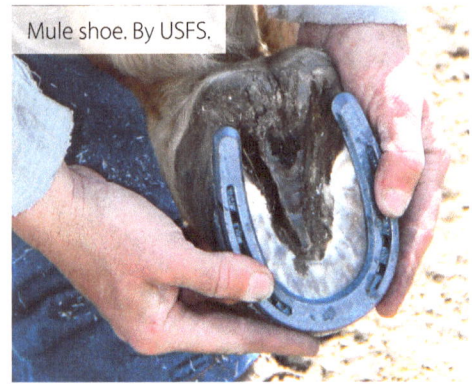

Mule shoe. By USFS.

Photo by Kari Greer.

Photo by USFS.

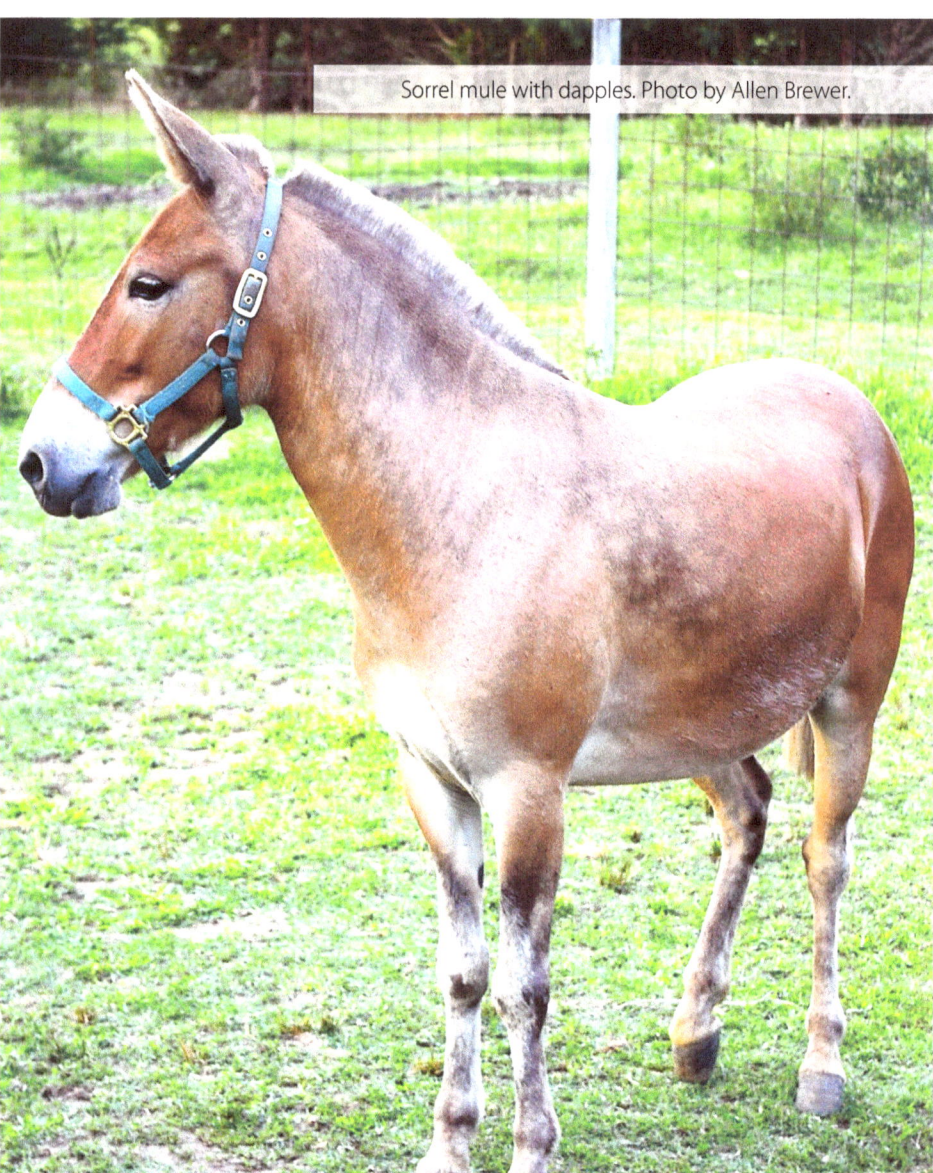

Sorrel mule with dapples. Photo by Allen Brewer.

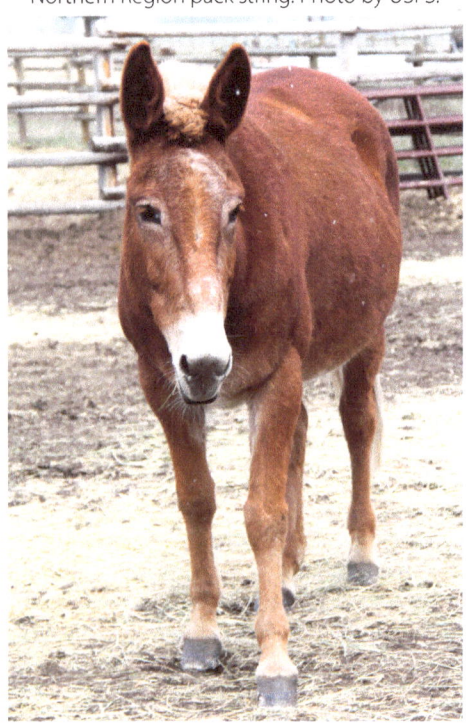

Sorrel mule from the U.S. Forest Service Northern Region pack string. Photo by USFS.

Sorrel draft mule.
Photo by U.S. National Park Service.

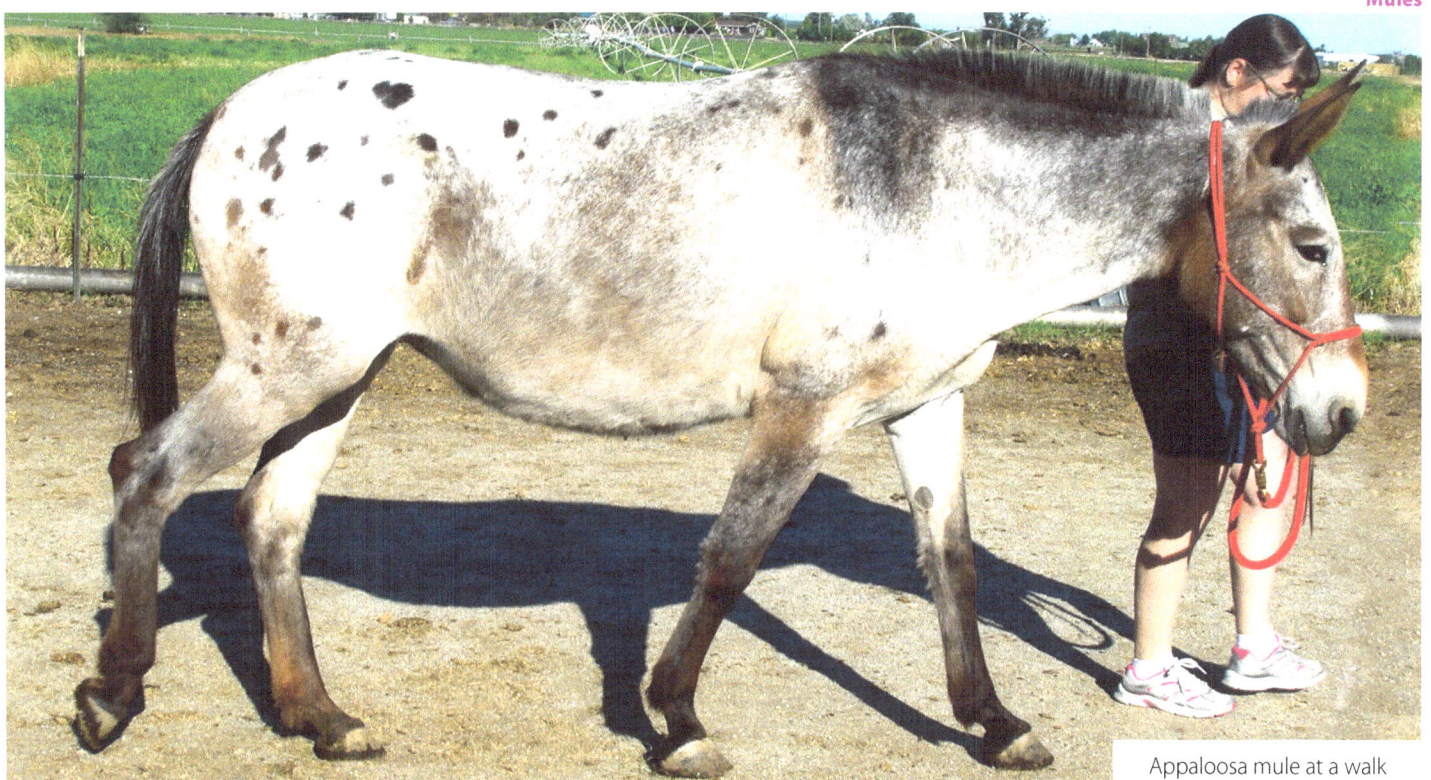

Appaloosa mule at a walk

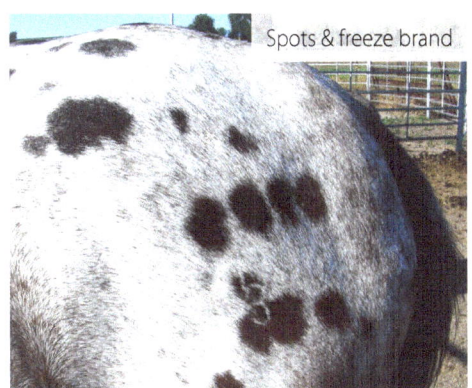

Spots & freeze brand

Forelock detail

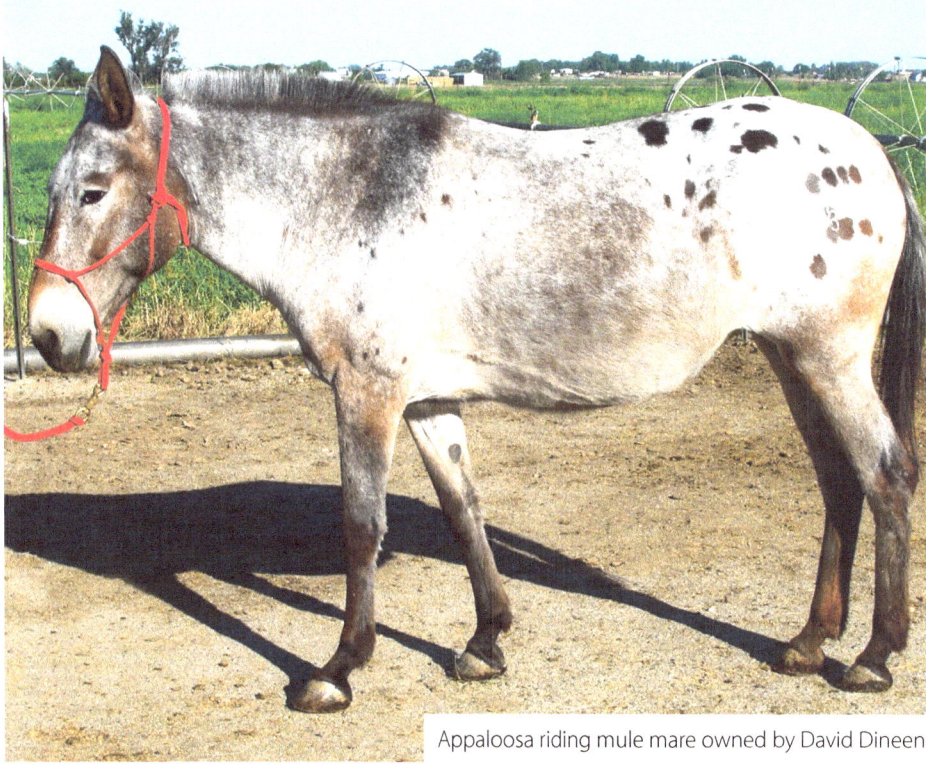

Appaloosa riding mule mare owned by David Dineen

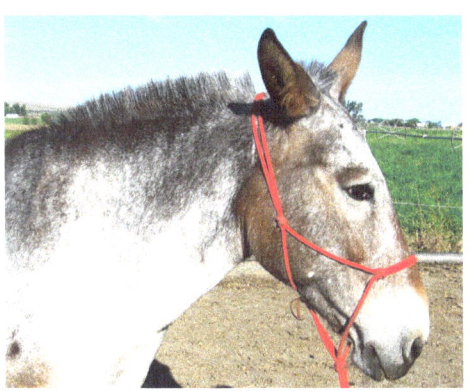

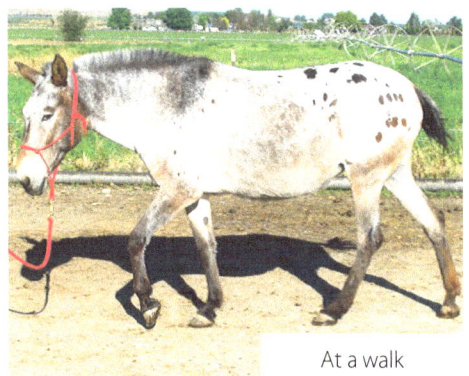

At a walk

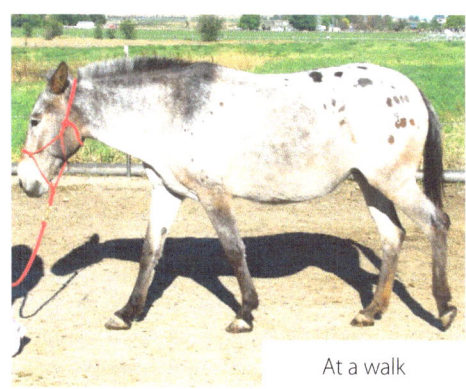

At a walk

Dun Fjord Mule Team for driving. Owned by David Dineen.

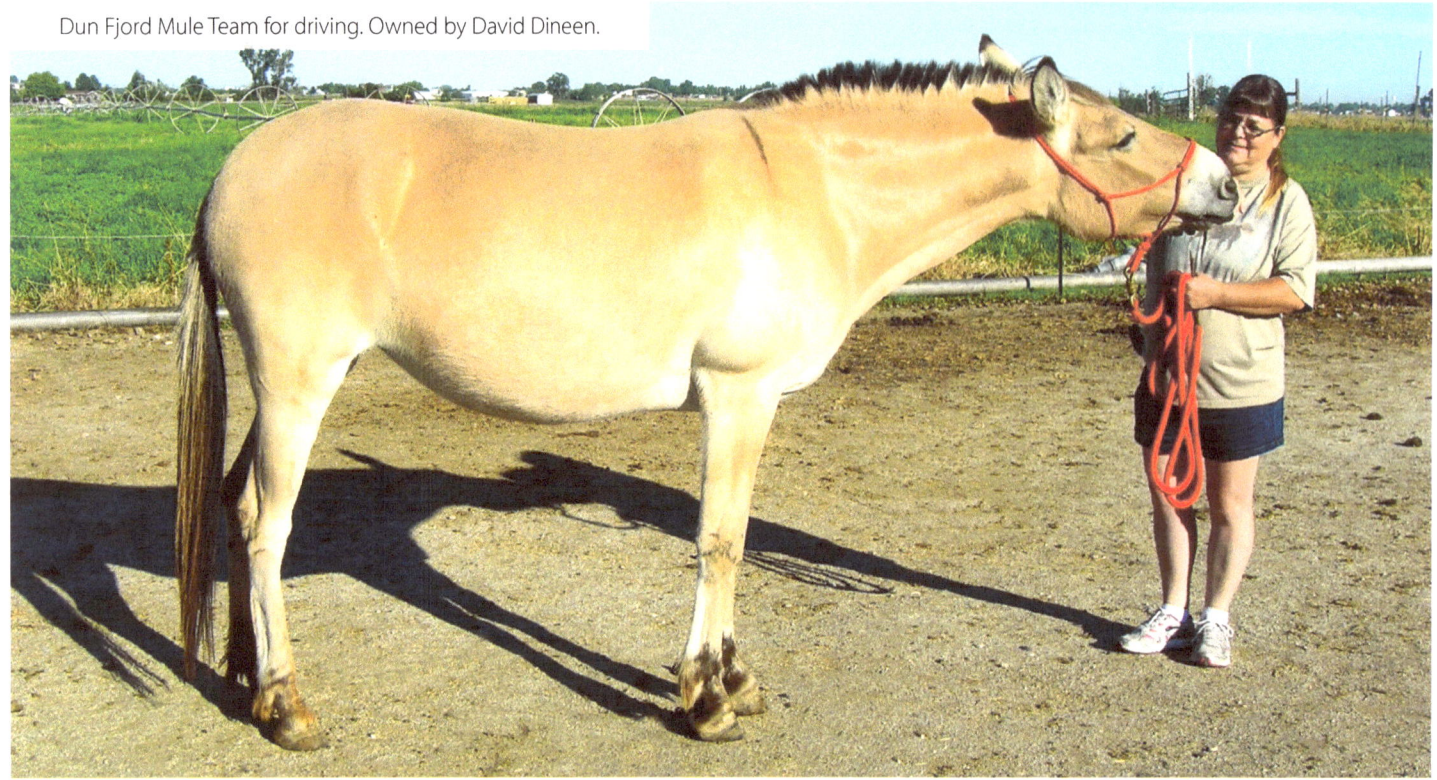

Valkyrie

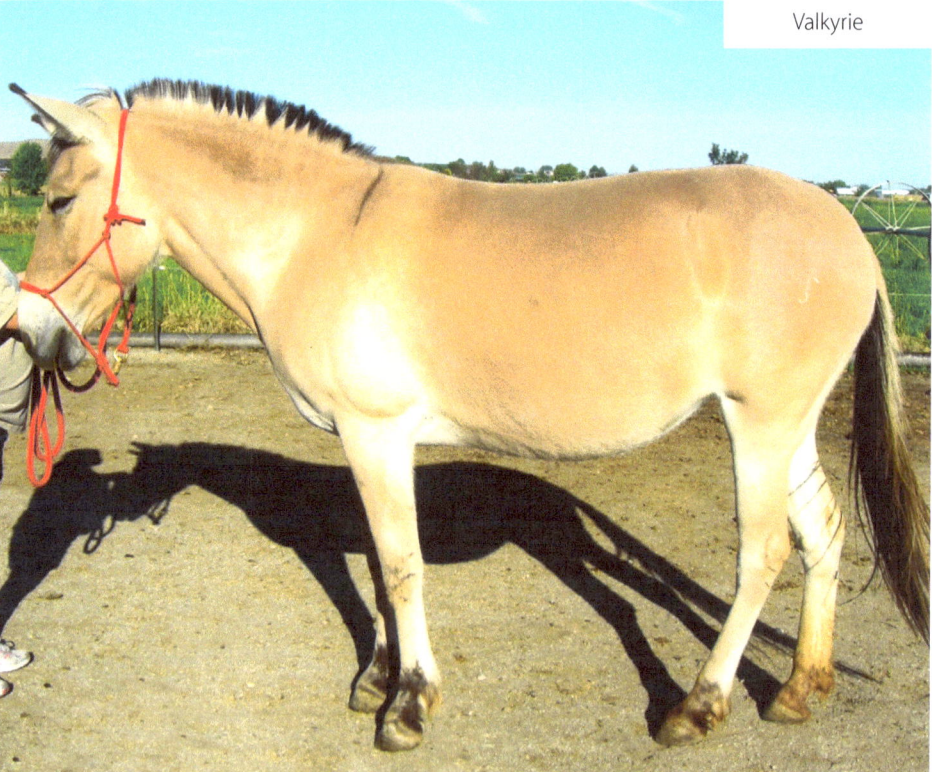

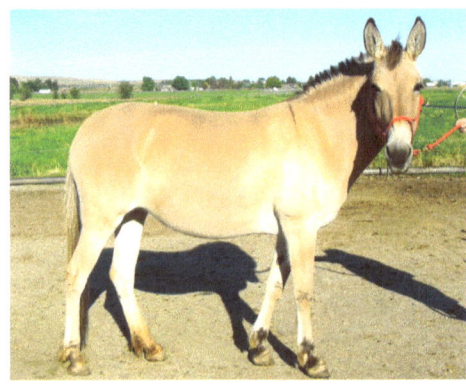

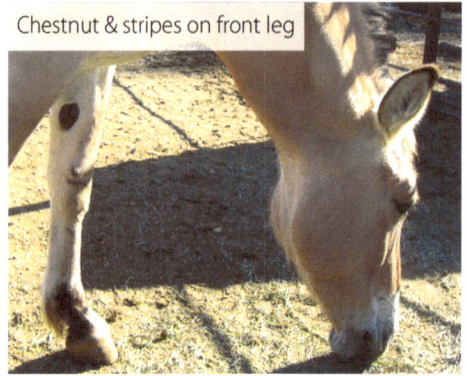

Chestnut & stripes on front leg

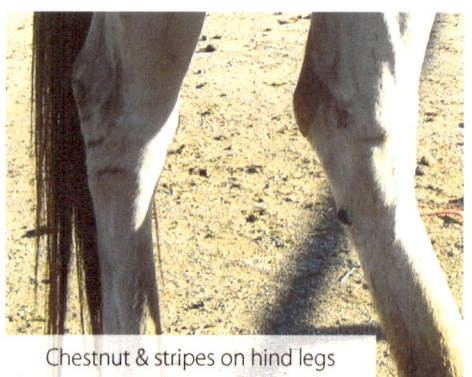

Chestnut & stripes on hind legs

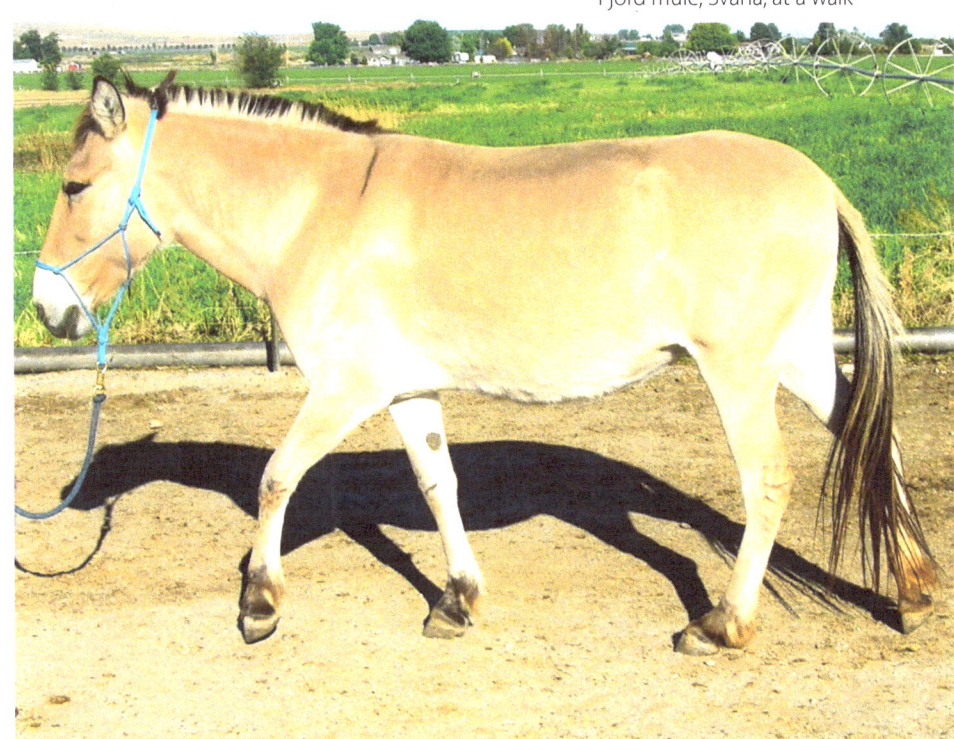

Fjord mule, Svana, at a walk

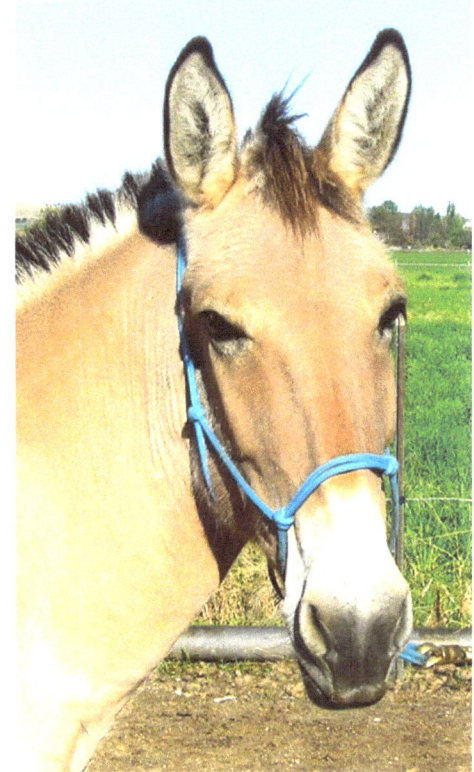

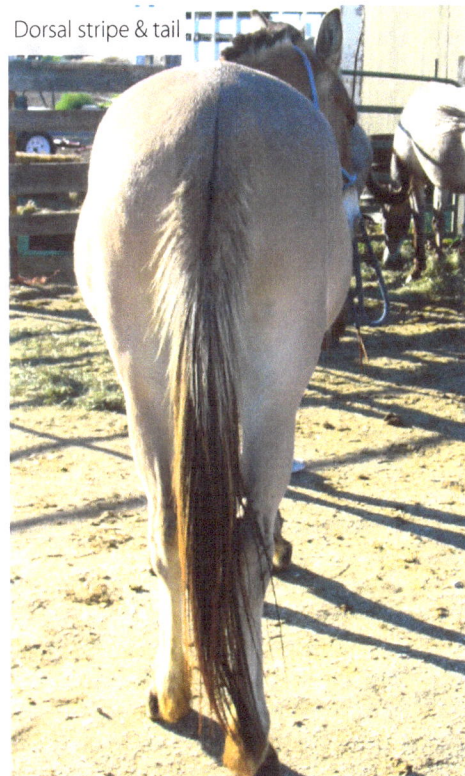

Dorsal stripe & tail

Shoulder bars, ear "stripes" & zig-zag manes

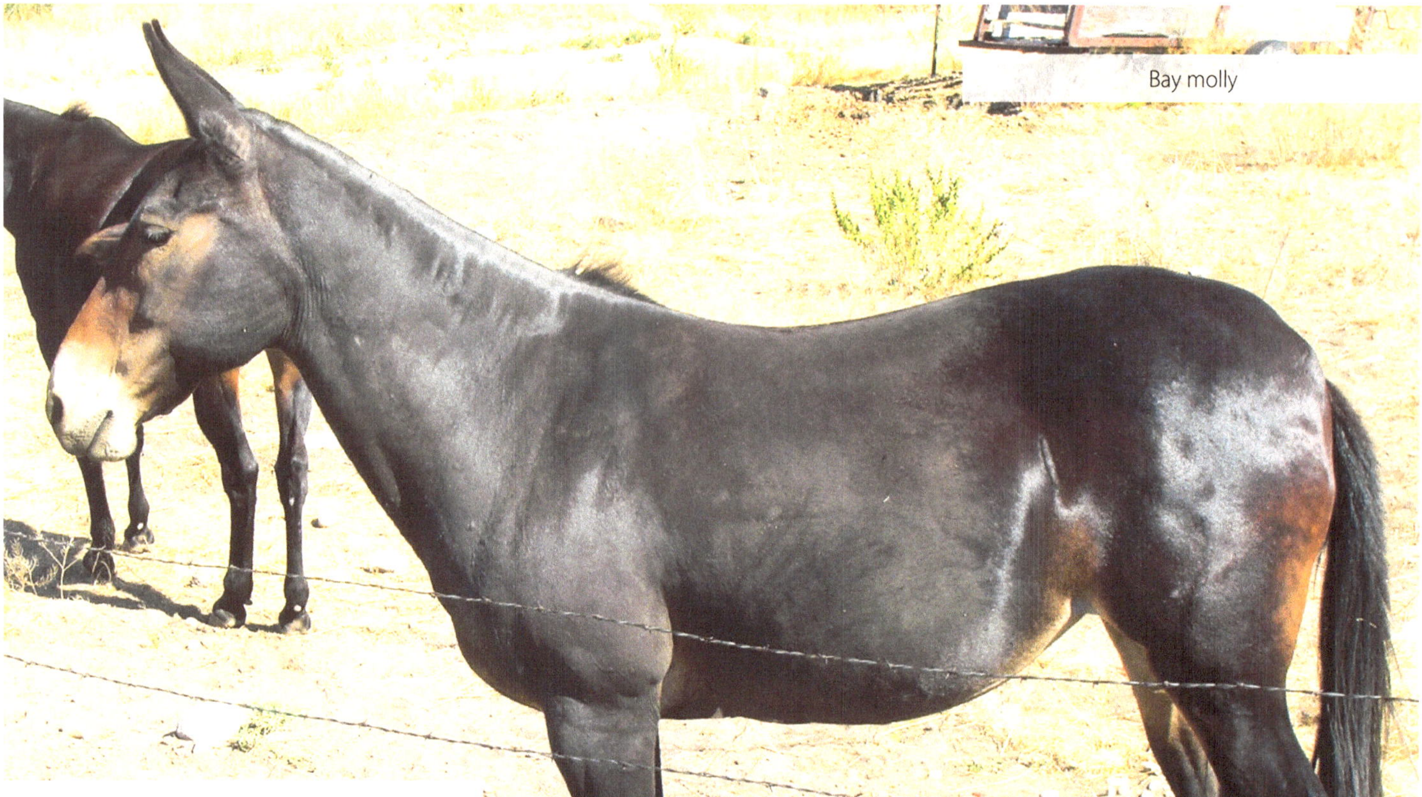

Bay molly

Bay Pinto Mule Team. Photo by Amanda Slater

Three abreast bay and liver chestnut mules

Bay draft mule team

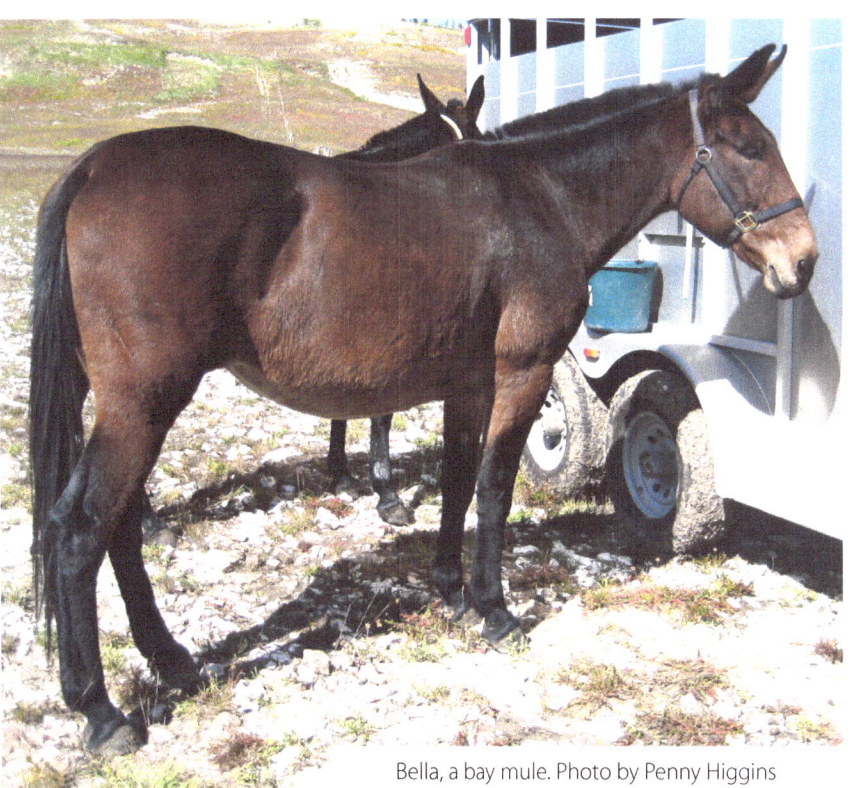

Bella, a bay mule. Photo by Penny Higgins

Red dun mule

Bay Appaloosa mule

Sorrel Belgian molly draft mules